**Human Body: an in**

Biology for K

- - - -   - - - -

©TazKai LLC

Photo Credits:

All photos are original photos taken by the author or rights purchased at Fotolia.com. All rights to appear in this book have been secured.

Some images within this book are either royalty-free images, used under license from their respective copyright holders, or images that are in the public domain. Images used under a creative commons license are duly attributed, and include a link to the relevant license, as per the author's instructions. All works in the public domain are considered public domain given life of the author plus 70 years or more as required by United States law.

**We have worked very hard to publish this book. Please leave a kind review in Amazon if you enjoy this ebook. If you have suggestions for us to improve please let us know in kind words so that we can improve our teaching resources.**

## About the Author

My name is Jon. I am a Registered Nurse on a Neurovascular Intensive Care Unit at a Level II Trauma Hospital in Dallas, TX. Health care and teaching are two of my passions in life and I love sharing the amazing story of the human body with others. I attended college at Brigham Young University and later received my Nursing degree at Methodist College in Peoria, IL. I love to run and exercise when I am not working in the hospital. I also hold a Business Management degree from Touro University.

## About this Book

This book is designed to provide children with a basic understanding of the major body systems including various things that can go wrong with the body. Each system is divided up into two sections; anatomy (structure) and physiology (function), and pathophysiology (what can go wrong). There are also basic questions for children to quiz themselves after completing a section to determine how much they have learned. For many people learning about the body is like learning a whole new language and the best way to remember the material is to review it often and make notes on the topics that are not as clear. With time anatomy and physiology will become second nature. I believe that the best way to understand the body, health care, and pathophysiology is to have a good understanding of the anatomy and physiology of the body. Once you know how things work it is easier to understand how things go wrong. This book is not a comprehensive biology text book, but will provide children with a great and enjoyable resource as they begin their study of the human body.

## Caution:

This ebook does contain some actual images of different organs from dissected animals including heart, lungs, kidneys. The images are clean and do not contain blood, but be advised if this might scare your child.

**We have worked very hard to publish this book. Please leave a kind review in Amazon if you enjoy this ebook. If you have suggestions for us to improve please let us know in kind words so that we can improve our teaching resources.**

# Contents

**The Heart**

Anatomy and Physiology

The heart is a muscle that pumps blood throughout the entire body, pumping an average of 70 times per minute every minute of a person's life. Think of the heart as a pump. Without the heart your body would not be able to move blood to all the other organs.

The heart sits behind the sternum in the chest cavity weighing about 1 pound and is only about the size of an adult fist.

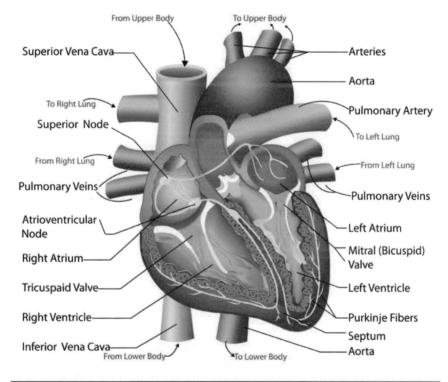

Surrounding the heart is a very thin layer called the **pericardium**. This layer protects the heart and aids in keeping it in place within the chest cavity.

Inside the heart are four hollow chambers. Two atria on the top and two **ventricles** on the bottom. It is best to think of the heart as having a right side and a left side. So the right side has an atrium on top and a ventricle on the bottom. The left side also has one atrium on top and a ventricle on the bottom.

Blood comes into the heart from the body into the right **atrium**. This blood is them pushed downward into the right ventricle. From the right ventricle the blood is pumped into the lungs. In the lungs the blood drops off carbon dioxide and picks up oxygen needed by all the body organs. Once it has received oxygen from the lungs the blood comes back into the heart through the left atrium. From the left atrium the blood is pumped down into the left ventricle. The left ventricle is the strongest chamber within the heart. The left ventricle pumps the blood out and into every artery in the body. From the left ventricle the blood exits the heart through the aorta and into the body's circulatory system. This cycle is repeated an average of 70 times per minute every single minute of your life!

Every minute your heart pumps about 4 to 8 liters of blood throughout the body. That is about 1 to 2 gallons each minute of life.

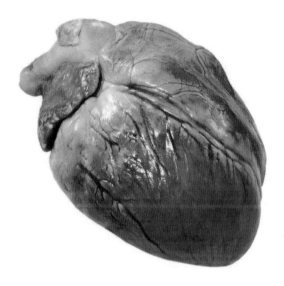

In order for your heart muscles to continue pumping, they require some sort of electrical charge to keep them moving. Heart muscles are different from the muscles of your arms or legs. If you want to pick up a drink with your arm, you actually have to think about it. That thought is then conducted to your brain which then sends electrical impulses to your arm to tell it to move. The muscles in your arms and legs are examples of skeletal muscles and they require thought and action to get them to move. The heart muscle is a special kind of muscle called cardiac muscle. You do not have to think about it or tell your heart to beat, it just does it all on its own! The electrical impulse that makes the muscles beat in your heart comes from a very specialized area located within the right atrium called **the SINOATRIAL NODE** or the SA Node. The SA node can create electrical currents that result in the heart pumping all on its own.

# Electrical System of the Heart

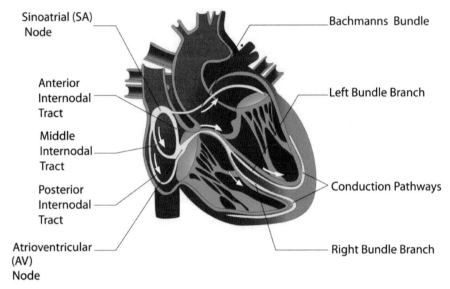

Sinoatrial (SA) Node

Bachmanns Bundle

Anterior Internodal Tract

Left Bundle Branch

Middle Internodal Tract

Posterior Internodal Tract

Conduction Pathways

Atrioventricular (AV) Node

Right Bundle Branch

When the SA Node sends an electrical current it causes the two atria to squeeze blood down into the ventricles. The electrical current then passes down into the **ATRIOVENTRICULAR NODE** or AV node where it then travels down the **Purkinje Fibers** (say that 10 times fast!). The Purkinje Fibers surround the muscles outside of the two lower ventricles. As the electrical current passes through the Purkinje Fibers it causes the ventricles to push the blood out. Remember the blood from the right ventricle moves into the lungs and the blood from the left ventricle goes up into the aorta and into the body. All of this happens very rapidly and blood in continually moving into the lungs to receive oxygen and into the body to deliver the blood and oxygen to the other organs.

As the blood is pumping in and out of the atria and ventricles it is important that it moves in the right direction and keeps moving forward. To keep the blood from moving backward there are special valves between the atria and the ventricles and between the right ventricle and the lungs and between the left ventricle and the aorta. These valves open and close based on the pressure of the blood within the chambers. As the chambers fill and the electrical current moves throughout the heart muscle the pressure builds and forces the valves to open or close. The valve between the right atrium and right ventricle is called the **TRICUSPID** valve. The valve between the left atrium and the left ventricle is called the **BICUSPID or MITRAL** valve. The valve between the right ventricle and the lungs is called the **PULMONARY** valve. And the valve between the left ventricle and the aorta is called the **AORTIC** valve. The "LUB" "DUB" sound and the feeling of your heart beating these valves closing as they push blood through the system. The "LUB" sound is the sound of the valves in the ventricles closing. The "DUB" sound is the valves in the atrium closing.

*End of Chapter Quiz*

1. Where does blood enter the heart?

2. Where does the electrical impulse that causes your heart to beat come from?

3. How much blood does the heart pump every minute?


Answers: right atrium, SA node, 4-8 liters

## The Circulatory System

Anatomy and Physiology

The Circulatory System is the transportation system of the body, carrying oxygen, nutrients and other essentials to the cells of the body while ferrying away toxic byproducts of cellular processes as well as excess heat. The red blood cells are the primary transportation vehicles. You can think of them like the mailmen of the body. In addition to the red blood cells, humans have white blood cells that are both the protectors and the doctors of the body. They seek and destroy foreign invaders as well as promote healing when we are injured.

The circulatory system looks and acts like the transportation infrastructure of your local township. There are the superhighways, or the veins and arteries, and then the more surface streets, or the capillaries. Arteries carry oxygen and nutrient rich blood away from the heart to the rest of the body while veins bring the spent blood back for recharging. Capillaries are simply smaller veins and arteries that can be found inside the organs and in locations where arteries turn into veins as blood begins its trip back to the heart.

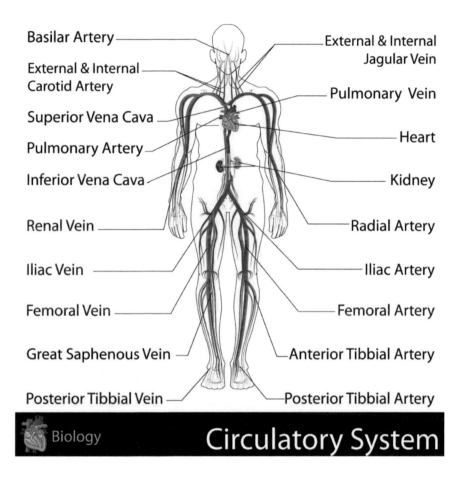

| Basilar Artery | External & Internal Jagular Vein |
| External & Internal Carotid Artery | Pulmonary Vein |
| Superior Vena Cava | Heart |
| Pulmonary Artery | |
| Inferior Vena Cava | Kidney |
| Renal Vein | Radial Artery |
| Iliac Vein | Iliac Artery |
| Femoral Vein | Femoral Artery |
| Great Saphenous Vein | Anterior Tibbial Artery |
| Posterior Tibbial Vein | Posterior Tibbial Artery |

**Biology** | **Circulatory System**

### The Heart

You can't discuss the circulatory system without starting with the heart. The heart is a four chambered muscle that is at the center of the circulatory system. The right side of the heart is called the low pressure side and is responsible for taking the blood returned by the veins back up to the lungs for recharging. Venous blood enters the heart in the right upper chamber known as the atrium. The heart pushes the blood into the right ventricle or lower chamber, which then pumps the blood through the pulmonary artery into the lungs for oxygenation. The tricuspid valve is the one way valve that sits between the right atrium and right ventricle that prevents the backflow of blood when the ventricle pumps the blood up to the lungs.

The blood then leaves the pulmonary artery and branches out into one of thousands of capillaries. In the capillaries, the blood is carried past tiny air sacs called alveoli, which transfer oxygen from the lungs to the red blood cells.

After the red blood cells have been reoxygenated, they move from the capillaries into veins known as the cardiac veins, where the blood is carried away from the lungs and into the left side of the heart. This is the high pressure side of the heart and it responsible for pushing the oxygenated blood from the heart back down into the body.

The reoxygenated blood enters the left side of the heart through the left atrium, or upper chamber. It is then pushed through the mitral valve into the left ventricle and then pumped out into the body. The mitral valve works in the same capacity as the tricuspid valve, preventing the backflow of blood as it is pumped out of the heart.

### The Aorta and the Arterial System

When the blood leaves the heart to head out into the body and begins delivering its packages, it leaves the heart in an artery known as the aorta. The **Aorta** is the largest artery in the body and is the transportation hub for the entire body. The aorta branches into smaller arteries that transport the oxygen rich blood to the body through a structure known as the aortic arch.

From the aorta, the oxygen rich blood is carried off to every single cell in the blood through a system of arteries and arterioles (smaller arteries) and then capillaries. After the blood passes through the capillaries and offloads its oxygen and nutrient payload, it heads back up to the heart through the veins in order to start the process completely over again.

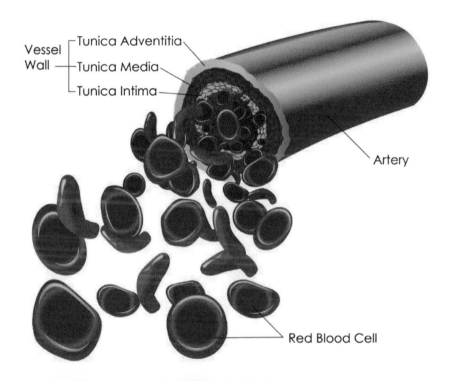

Vessel Wall
- Tunica Adventitia
- Tunica Media
- Tunica Intima

Artery

Red Blood Cell

 Biology                    **Red Blood Cells**

**The Venous System**

The **venous system** is the opposite of the arterial system. It collects the deoxygenated blood through a system of ever increasing sized vessels in order to return it to the heart and lungs. The blood passes through the capillaries and moves to larger vessels known as vennules and is then carried to the veins. The two largest veins are the **superior and inferior vena cava**. The superior vena cava is responsible for moving the blood from the upper half of the body to the right atrium and the inferior vena cava is responsible for transporting the blood from the lower half of the body to the heart.

And then the process starts all over again in the right atrium. The human circulatory system is considered a closed system because the blood is contained in a series of vessels.

**All About Atherosclerosis**

Blood vessels should be stretchy when they are working correctly. Imagine that as time passes sticky objects start to build up and clog these "tubes." Because the blood vessels are clogged the nutrients are not able to pass through, so they start to harden. This is basically what happens with **atherosclerosis**. Problems that deal with the disease depend on where in your body the vessel hardening is happening.

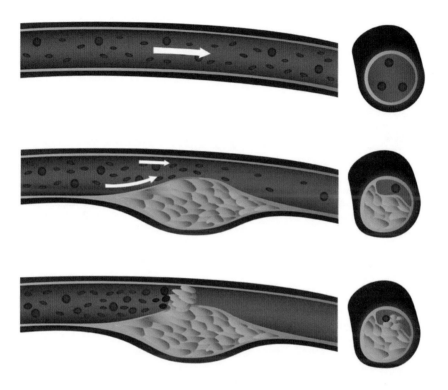

Remember, atherosclerosis is a preventable and treatable condition. Sometimes, changing the things you do on a regular basis is the best treatment for atherosclerosis. **Eating healthier and exercising daily can help slow or even stop the disease from growing**. If those things don't work, your doctor may suggest surgery to slow the disease.

Some medication can slow or even sometimes undo the effects of atherosclerosis. Examples of regularly used medications are:

- Cholesterol medications: Quickly lowering the amount of *bad cholesterol* can stop or even undo the "tubes" from clogging. The drugs are known as statins and fibrates.

- Anti-platelet medications: These are used to reduce the chance that the clumping will happen and cause even more clogging.

- Beta blocker medications: They slow down your heart beat which lowers the amount of work your heart has to do. This usually will make your chest pains go away. Beta blockers lower the chance of heart attacks and heart rhythm problems.

- Angiotensin-converting enzyme (ACE) inhibitors: These help slow the disease down by lowering blood pressure and helping the "tubes" that need to transport nutrients throughout your body to have a clog-free flow. ACE inhibitors can also lower consistent heart attacks.

- Calcium channel blockers: These help lower blood pressure and are sometimes used to treat a type of chest pains called *angina*.

- Water pills (or diuretics): These help lower blood pressure.

- Other medications: Your doctor may tell you about certain medications to control other parts of your body that deal with atherosclerosis, like diabetes. Also, specific medications may be used to help treat the signs of the disease, such as pain relievers for people who experience arm pain during exercise.

Learn more by watching these colorful videos!!!
Below are links to a few educational videos on atherosclerosis uploaded by the Khan Academy:
Atherosclerosis (Part 1)
Atherosclerosis (Part 2)

1. Where do red blood cells get oxygen?

2. What do anti-platelet medications do?

3. What are the two largest veins?


Answers: alveoli, prevent blood from clotting and clogging, superior and inferior vena cava

## The Brain

### Anatomy and Physiology

The brain is an organ of the human body located in the skull. This organ is responsible for all the thoughts, feelings, and memories a person has. It also provides the commands for various bodily functions like breathing. It's often compared to a computer, but there are two major differences. First, a computer consists of discrete components that produce electrical outputs, while the brain consists of cells called neurons that generate chemical outputs. Second, a computer operates according to a software program that's well-understood. The ways in which the brain produces thoughts and makes decisions are not fully understood.

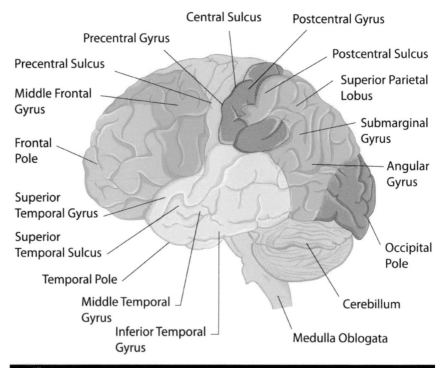

 Biology                    Brain Anatomy

In an average adult, the brain weighs about three pounds and has a roughly oval shape that tappers toward the front. The overall dimensions are 6.5 inches long by 5.5 inches wide by 3.6 inches high. The brain comprises only 2% of the body's total weight, but consumes over 20% of all the calories the body uses (calories are what provides the body with energy to move and operate). The most basic parts of the brain are its **neurons or nerve cells**. There are around **100 billion of them**. Instead of making direct physical contact, neurons send signals to each other by producing chemicals called **neurotransmitters** that fill gaps called synapses between neurons. When a neurotransmitter touches another neuron, it develops an electric charge that triggers its own neurotransmitters. These, in turn, pass the signal on to the next neuron. This method allows the nerve cells to rearrange themselves when new information is being generated or stored in the brain.

The brain itself consists of several distinct components. At the bottom center is the **brain stem**. This part acts as a gateway between the higher regions of the brain and the spinal cord. It also handles involuntary operations like breathing, body temperature, and coughing, among others. Above this, the **cerebellum** organizes muscle activities and maintains balance. Covering these two regions, the **cerebrum** carries out the more advanced thought processes. This region possesses roughly 2.5 square feet of tissue, but it contains multiple wrinkles that allow it to fit inside the skull. The outer surface that performs complex thought is called the **cerebral cortex**.

The cerebrum is divided into two hemispheres joined together by a cluster of fibers called the corpus callosum. In addition, the cerebrum is subdivided into four lobes. The **frontal lobe**, at the front, handles executive functions like judging, organizing, personality, and focusing. It also produces complex speech and controls deliberate bodily movements. The **parietal lobe**, on the top, interprets bodily sensations and assists in comprehending sights and sounds. The temporal lobe, on the side, works to understand language and help with memory and sounds. Finally, the occipital lobe, at the back, is exclusively devoted to processing visual information.

http://www.youtube.com/watch?v=JQEiux-AOzs

Sympathetic and Parasympathetic Nervous Systems

Along with the higher regions of the brain, there are structures located at the base of it that handle more primitive actions. The **limbic system** produces more basic emotions than the higher brain. This allows it to make quick decisions about events taking place around a person. It does this with little input from the conscious brain. This system is made up of the **hypothalamus**, the **hippocampus, and the amygdala**. When this system is triggered, it sends signals to the brain stem. This, in turn, activates the **sympathetic nervous system**. This is the part of the spinal cord that stimulates various organs in the body to prepare for possible self-defense or escape, also called the fight or flight response. Several important actions are triggered by the sympathetic nervous system. The heart begins beating faster so that more oxygen is delivered to the muscles. The breathing rate increases so that more oxygen can enter the blood stream. The adrenal glands are stimulated to produce adrenalin. Blood is diverted to the main muscle groups. This system also causes the pupils of the eyes to dilate and the sweat glands to produce fluid.

# Sympathetic System

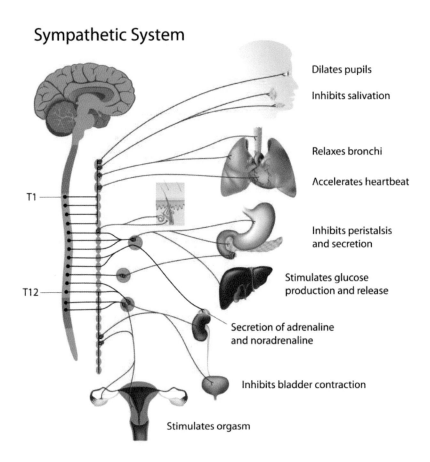

Dilates pupils

Inhibits salivation

Relaxes bronchi

Accelerates heartbeat

T1

Inhibits peristalsis and secretion

Stimulates glucose production and release

T12

Secretion of adrenaline and noradrenaline

Inhibits bladder contraction

Stimulates orgasm

Once a crisis situation is dealt with, the body needs to return to a resting state. If it remains agitated for too long, muscles and organs can be damaged. **The parasympathetic nervous system** handles this task. It is strongly controlled by the limbic system, too. When this system is activated, air flow in the lungs is decreased. This forces the person to breathe slower. It also reduces heart rate, constricts the pupils of the eyes, and produces saliva in the mouth. All of this happens more slowly than the initial response of the sympathetic system. After things have settled down, the hypothalamus in the limbic system keeps the body's basic functions operating evenly. This is referred to as homeostasis. Additionally, the hypothalamus oversees sensations like hunger, thirst, pain, pleasure, and anger.

# Parasympathetic System

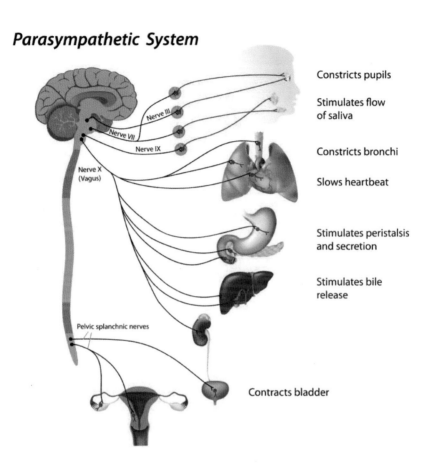

Constricts pupils

Stimulates flow of saliva

Constricts bronchi

Slows heartbeat

Stimulates peristalsis and secretion

Stimulates bile release

Contracts bladder

Nerve III

Nerve VII

Nerve IX

Nerve X (Vagus)

Pelvic splanchnic nerves

**Major Disorder of the Brain**
**Stroke**

A stroke occurs when the blood flow to the brain is slowed down or interrupted. The blood vessels in the brain become starved for oxygen and other nutrients to help it continue to flow. As a result there the symptoms begin quickly. Symptoms include but are not limited to weakness, numbness, paralysis, slurred speech, aphasia (unable to speak), and problems with vision.

There are two different types of strokes. One is called **ischemic**. An ischemic stroke is caused when the arteries in the brain are blocked. This will cause the fresh blood that comes from the heart and lungs to stop moving and deposit the cellular waste and carbon dioxide. The second kind of stroke is called a **hemorrhagic stroke**. A hemorrhagic stroke occurs when a blood vessel bursts in the brain and blood surrounds brain tissue compressing it tightly.

Most diseases that cause a stroke are attributed to the heart and blood vessels. Such conditions include heart disease, high blood pressure, Coronary artery disease, and other diseases that affect the blood flow to the brain.

Strokes occur to people who are over the age of 55. The risk of having a stroke is higher in males than females. There is also a higher risk in African-American, Hispanic, and Asian-Pacific people than any other ethnicity. People who have a history of stroke in their family are also a higher risk as are people who have diabetes.

There are many clot-busting drugs that can be administered within about 4 hours through the veins in the brain. The quicker the drug is administered, the better it will work. Medications such as Warfarin or other anti-platelet drugs help to end a stroke. Stents can be inserted to help unblock an artery in the brain as well.

Here is a video that helps you understand how a stroke works. All about a stroke

# Brain Stroke

### Ischemic Stroke

### Hemorrhagic Stroke

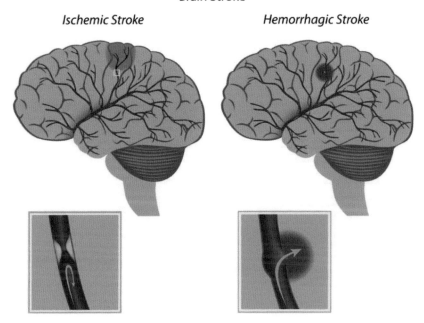

Blockage of blood vessels; lack of blood flow to affected area

Rupture of blood vessels; leakage of blood

*End of Chapter Quiz*

1. Describe the difference between the sympathetic and parasympathetic nervous systems.

2. Describe the difference between an ischemic and hemorrhagic stroke.

**The Digestive System**

Anatomy and Physiology

The digestive system can be thought of as a converter. It mechanically and chemically converts proteins, fats and carbohydrates into absorbable forms to be used by the body for energy, growth and repair.

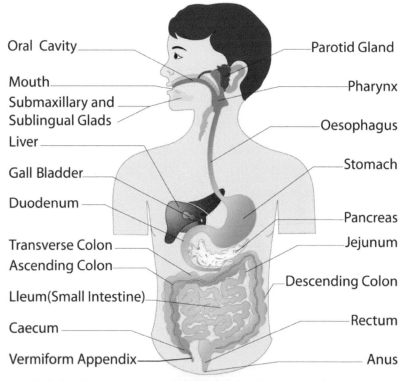

Oral Cavity

Mouth

Submaxillary and
Sublingual Glads

Liver

Gall Bladder

Duodenum

Transverse Colon

Ascending Colon

Lleum(Small Intestine)

Caecum

Vermiform Appendix

Parotid Gland

Pharynx

Oesophagus

Stomach

Pancreas

Jejunum

Descending Colon

Rectum

Anus

Biology                    Digestive System

The digestive system has several organs: the stomach, liver, gallbladder, pancreas and the small and large intestines. The complete digestive system begins at the mouth and ends at the anus. The digestive system end to end is called the alimentary canal.

In your mouth food is mechanically broken down by your teeth. The tongue helps food stay between your teeth and contains taste buds so you can experience flavors. Salivary glands in your mouth secrete saliva to moisten food for swallowing and begins the digestive (breaking down) process of food. The **pharynx** is a muscular tube located at the back of your mouth. It connects the mouth to the esophagus and helps to swallow food.

Your **esophagus** is located behind the trachea and between the lungs. It is a tube about 10 inches long and an inch in diameter. It carries food from the pharynx to the stomach . Muscles in the esophagus push food along. Where the esophagus meets the **stomach** is a ring of muscle called a **sphincter**. It allows food to enter the stomach and closes to prevent food backing up into the esophagus.

The **stomach** is below the lungs. It is a saclike organ about the size of your fist. It has two openings, one from the esophagus and the other to the small intestine. Sphincters at each end of the stomach keep food in the stomach while it is being digested. The stomach wall is comprised of muscle and an inner lining called the **rugae**. The rugae has folds that expand as we eat more. **The stomach can expand 10 times it's size!** Rugae secretes hydrochloric acid to chemically start converting solid food into a liquid called **chyme**. The stomach's lower sphincter opens to allow chyme into the small intestine.

The **small intestine** is positioned below the stomach. It is about 20 feet long and about 1 inch in diameter. It extends from the stomach to the large intestine. The inside has a large surface area due to many folds of the mucosa. These folds are called **villi**. The liver, gallbladder and pancreas deliver enzymes which convert the nutrients in the chyme to amino acids and sugars before being absorbed by the villi. Any undigested material from the small intestine is passed along to the large intestine.

The **large intestine** is found above and on two sides of the small intestines. It is about 5 feet long and about 2.5 inches in diameter. No digestion occurs in the large intestine, just absorption of water and vitamins produced by bacteria that normally live in the large intestine. All leftover waste material moves from the large intestine to the anus, the last section of the digestive system.

This material is eliminated from the anus as feces.

**Peptic Ulcers**

As an integral part of the functioning of our digestive system our bodies produce acids to assist in the dissolving of food. For various reasons sometimes our bodies build an overabundance of these acids. Normally we have a built in defense in the form of a thin layer of mucous that lines the walls of the digestive track. However, as the build-up of acids increases, it overtakes this defense and starts to eat at the lining of the digestive tract; this is what is known as a **peptic ulcer**. The acid leaves open sores that can cause severe pain and disruption of normal digestive processes. Patients suffering from peptic ulcers most commonly report a burning pain anywhere from the middle of their chest to the navel. Patients may also experience frequent vomiting with blood, changes in appetite and weight loss.

# Peptic Ulcer

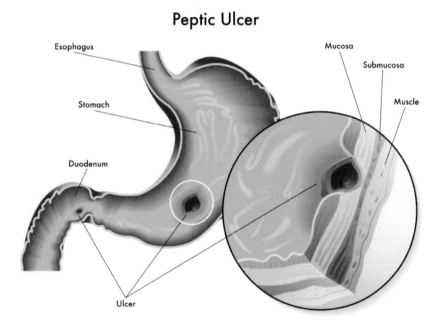

Originally the cause of these sores was thought to be related to stress and diet. Doctors now know that most of these ulcers form because of over the counter medications like Aspirin and Ibuprofen, and because of bacterial infections. One type that doctors have associated with peptic ulcers is the Helicobacter pylori bacteria. This bacterium commonly lives within the lining of our digestive tracts without causing any issues, but can sometimes be associated with inflammation of the lining; which can lead to ulcers. The medications that we take frequently to relieve the body of pain (like a headache) can also lead to inflammation if not used properly and sparingly.

Peptic ulcers are easily treatable with acid production blocking medications and/or an antibiotic to kill bacterium. Ulcers are easily preventable by using over the counter pain medications responsibly and, by taking steps to protect your body against bacteria and infections.

*End of Chapter Activity*
1. On a sheet of paper draw the digestive system from the mouth to the anus and label all parts.

**The Liver**

Anatomy and Physiology

The human liver is located in the right and upper quadrant of the abdomen. For a better frame of reference, the liver is located right above the diaphragm behind the rib cage. The liver is attached to the abdominal wall and the diaphragm. This attachment divides the liver into a large right lobe and a small left lobe.

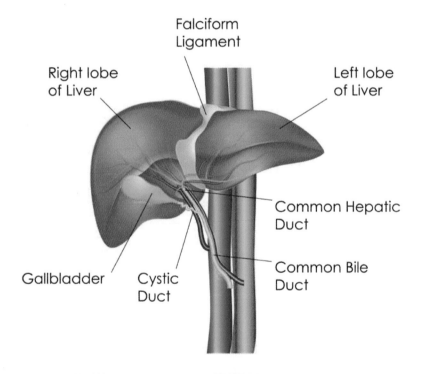

Falciform Ligament

Right lobe of Liver

Left lobe of Liver

Common Hepatic Duct

Common Bile Duct

Gallbladder

Cystic Duct

 Biology

Liver Anatomy

Though the liver is responsible for the biotransformation of toxins, drugs, and hormones and other functions, it is a relatively small and only comprises approximately two percent of the total human body's weight.

Not only does the liver clear red blood cells and bacteria by phagocytosis, but it also manages nutrients and synthesizes plasma proteins such as protein C, globulin, and insulin-like growth factor. It also plays a role in clotting, phagocytosis, and vitamin and mineral storage.

Glisson's capsule can be found on the surface of the liver. This is a connective tissue layer that will extend into the liver except for the smallest vessels. In the late 1950s, a French surgeon by the name of Claude Couinaud described 8 liver segments. Later studies revealed that there may be as many as twenty segments. Each segment has its own independent vascular and biliary branches.

When patients are diagnosed with cancer of the liver and need tumor removal, these segments become important as a basis for tumor removal. When performing segmental resection, blood loss is minimized when cancers are removed or disseminated via the portal vein. Normal livers are repaired with segmental resection.

Each segment of the liver is a separated lobules, which can be represented by various hepatocytes that radiate from a central vein. At the periphery, the lobules are served by venous, arterial, and biliary vessels. The lobules are connected by a small amount of connective tissue.

Nearly 75 percent of the blood flowing through the liver originates in **the portal vein**. The other 25 percent originates from the **hepatic artery**. Every minute, about 1.5 liters of blood exits the liver. Macrophage or reticuloendothelial cells found in the liver are responsible for clearing pathogens and debris from the liver. Since the average lifespan of a red blood cell is 120 days, dead and damaged cells will pass through the liver within this time frame.

Iron in the liver is transported by **transferrin**. Iron is an important part of the body's proper biological function and is useful in preventing syncope, lethargy, and other adverse reactions. Not only does the liver store iron, but it also stores other vitamins and minerals. In fact, 80 percent of the body's vitamin A storage is located in the liver within the stellate cells.

If there is enough vitamin A stored in the liver, there should be enough to prevent a deficiency for about 10 months. The liver can also hold vitamin B12 for approximately a year and vitamin D for about three to four months. Small amounts of vitamin E and vitamin K may also be found stored in the liver.

The liver receives a variety of lipid (fat) forms. Some of the most common lipid forms include chylomicrons remnants, low density lipoproteins (LDL), high density lipoproteins (HDL), and lipoprotein lipase (LPL). LPL proteins are often expressed on the endothelium of vessels.

The liver is an important aspect of the body that should be monitored to ensure proper functionality. Review the various aspects of the liver to ensure homeostasis within the body.

**References:**
http://www.youtube.com/user/liverdiseasecures
www.youtube.com/watch?v=RsPzIqcVaoY

*End of Chapter Quiz*

1. What is the biggest vein in the liver?

2. How is iron transferred?

Answers:  portal vein, transferrin

**The Pancreas**

The pancreas is a large, long, irregularly shaped organ located across the upper abdomen, behind the stomach. It is from 4 - 7 inches long and weighs about 3 ounces. The pancreas is a compound gland which is a member of two important systems in the body - the **digestive system and the endocrine system** - which means that it is an exocrine gland (secretes enzymes to the digestive system to help break down food) and an endocrine gland (secretes hormones directly into the blood stream to regulate blood sugars). Its main purpose is to help with digestion and blood sugar levels.

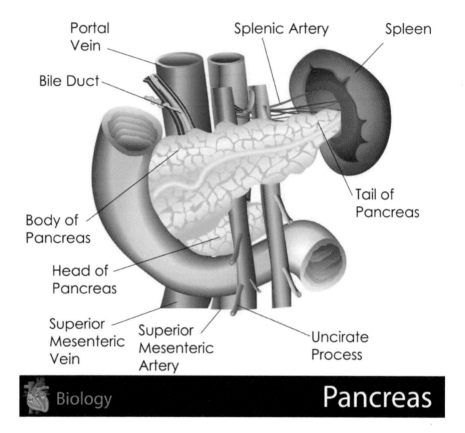

Portal Vein

Splenic Artery

Spleen

Bile Duct

Body of Pancreas

Head of Pancreas

Tail of Pancreas

Superior Mesenteric Vein

Superior Mesenteric Artery

Uncirate Process

Biology

# Pancreas

As an **endocrine gland**, it secretes hormones such as insulin, glucagon, and somatostatin directly into the bloodstream. Tiny island-like glandular cells, called the **Islets of Langerhans**, are responsible for producing the insulin and hormones that are released into the bloodstream to regulate blood sugar.

As an **exocrine gland**, it discharges digestive enzymes and pancreatic juices into the small intestine that assist in absorption of nutrients, and helps to break down proteins, carbohydrates, sugars, fats, and partially digested food between the stomach and the small intestine. In order to protect the intestinal lining, sodium bicarbonate is dispensed into the intestines, neutralizing excess stomach acid.

The pancreas has four parts - the head, neck, body, and a pointed tail. The head is located in the upper section of the small intestine and surrounds the bile duct; the neck is the thin part between the head and body; the body and tail cross the spine to the left; the point of the tail is near the spleen. The general location of the pancreas is behind the stomach, to the left of your diaphragm, right behind the left kidney. The body and neck drains into the vein that allows blood to drain from the spleen, or splenic vein. The head drains into the vessel that drains blood from the small intestine and directs blood to the intestines, spleen, and liver.

FUN FACTS ABOUT PANCREAS
• Greek anatomist Herophilus, who died in 280 B.C., was the first scientist to recognize the pancreas. Many years later, another anatomist, Rufus of Ephesus, was the one who gave the pancreas its name.
• The word pancreas is of Greek origin. Due to its flesh-like texture, the Greek terms were "whole flesh."
• Some vertebrate animals may have up to three pancreases.
• The pancreatic tissue of a rabbit is distributed throughout the other organs.

**For more information, check out these videos:**
o What Is a Pancreas? http://www.youtube.com/watch?v=1l2GTGEwZOY
o The Pancreas Song http://www.youtube.com/watch?v=c_RCEUNmsAc

Major Disorders of the Pancreas
**Understanding Type II Diabetes**

Type II diabetes is a condition that occurs when the body is not able to utilize insulin to aid in food digestion. Diabetes Type II is a metabolic disorder that begins with insulin resistance and leads to a combination of resistance and deficiency to insulin. More than 90% of all cases of diabetes are Type II. This condition is predisposed by genetics or can occur when a person develops obesity or other causes of resistance.

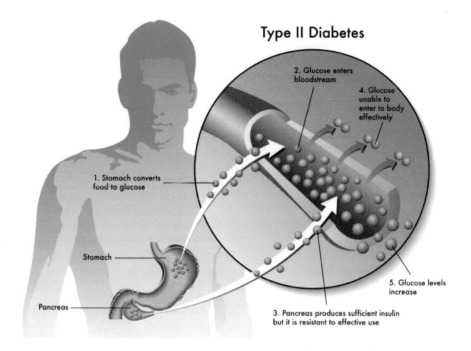

# Type II Diabetes

1. Stomach converts food to glucose

2. Glucose enters bloodstream

3. Pancreas produces sufficient insulin but it is resistant to effective use

4. Glucose unable to enter to body effectively

5. Glucose levels increase

Stomach

Pancreas

**The Basic Treatments of Disease**

Treating diabetes can be a complex balance between medication and diet. The first thing a doctor asks a patient with higher blood sugar is to do a reduced carb and sugar laden diet. If the sugar or glucose levels cannot be controlled with diet, then the next step will be to add anti-diabetic medications to their regime. These medications basically work inside the body to reduce the sugar in the blood and allow the body to work properly. If these types of medication are no longer effective, then insulin is administered by a shot. This instantly lowers the sugar levels and is reserved as a last resort for treatment of diabetes type II.

**Symptoms of Diabetes**

The first sign that someone has diabetes is increased thirst. Another warning sign that something is not right in the body is cuts that don't heal properly and may not heal at all. Other signs are frequent urination and a dizzy or lightheaded feeling. By conducting sugar checks with a glucometer at home, it is easy to get a pattern of where the glucose levels are in the body and report to the doctor.

## Complications Of The Condition

When the body has an overabundance of sugar in the blood, it can cause damage to major organs. Those fighting with diabetes can have problems with nerve pain and experience the feeling of pins and needles. Many people need to have limbs amputated because the blood flow decreases to the area becomes necrotic and dies. If the tissue dies, it can affect the whole body and the body can become septic and this can be deadly. However, with the advances in modern medicine, this is rarely the case these days. By following the doctor's orders, diabetes can be managed.

*End of Chapter Activity*
1. Describe the difference between an endocrine and an exocrine gland.

**Renal System (The Kidneys)**

**Anatomy and Physiology**
While they're vital to several bodily functions, the kidneys are primarily designed to filter harmful materials from the blood. They perform this work as part of the urinary tract. There are two of these fist-sized organs in the body. Their basic shape is like an oval that's been partially bent in half. In fact, kidney beans get their name from their very close resemblance to these organs. The pit in the midsection of each kidney is called the hilus. It's here that blood flows into the kidney through the renal artery and exits through the renal vein. The kidneys receive about **20% of the blood expelled by every beat of the heart**.

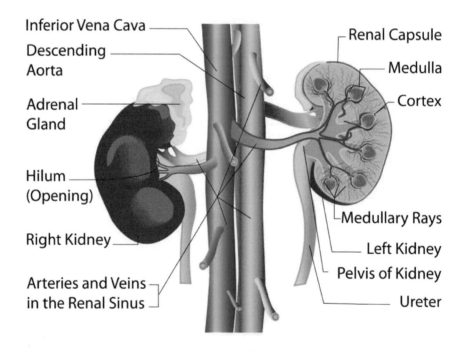

Once blood enters a kidney, it flows into separate filtering compartments called **nephrons**. There are about 1 million of these in a kidney. These nephrons are mainly located in the outer layer of the kidney called the **cortex**. Inside the nephron, the blood flows through a cluster of very small capillaries called a **glomerulus**. The capillaries have pores in them that allow contaminants and water to pass through while blocking red blood cells. The water and impurities are collected by a surrounding structure called **bowman's capsule**. From bowman's capsule, the wastes pass through a tubule.

During this filtering process, the kidneys also allow nutrients back into the blood. Once this operation is done, the remaining waste accumulates in the renal pyramids. Between 10 and 15 of these structures are located toward the interior of the kidney called the **medulla**. This mixture of wastes and water, called urine, is then deposited in funnel-like features called **calyxes**. It's then concentrated in the renal pelvis that sends it out of the kidney through the **ureter**. The ureter emerges from the hilus and links to the bladder.

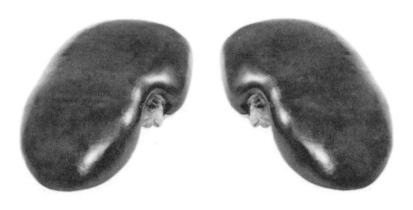

The kidney doesn't just filter materials out of the blood. It also regulates how much water, salt and other chemicals are in the blood. The **tubules** are located next to the capillaries that carry blood back out from the nephrons. It's at this point that water, salt, glucose, and minerals are reabsorbed into the blood according to various hormonal signals received by the kidney. **This maintenance of water and nutrients is another of the kidney's vital functions.** Using water as one example, other areas of the body, like the pituitary gland and hypothalamus, are able to determine if there's too much or too little water available. As water levels drop, the pituitary produces a hormone called **ADH** that causes the tubules and other components of the kidneys to let more water pass back into the blood stream.

Just as the kidneys can respond to hormone signals from elsewhere, they are also able to detect problems and release their own hormones. When oxygen levels in the blood start to drop, the kidneys detect this and produce a hormone called **erythropoietin**. This hormone stimulates the production of new red blood cells. The process itself is called **erythropoiesis**. The kidneys also can respond to lowered blood pressure by releasing an enzyme called **renin**. This enzyme triggers a series of reactions that ultimately cause blood vessels to narrow and increase pressure. This action, along with generating new blood cells and regulating water levels, makes the kidneys a key part of determining blood pressure.

*End of Chapter Quiz*

1. What are two primary functions of the kidneys?

2. What is the process called whereby red blood cells are created?

Answers: filtering blood, maintaining fluid balance, erythropoiesis

## Respiratory System

### Anatomy and Physiology

"That's as natural as breathing," goes the old expression. While breathing is indeed so natural that we hardly think about it – do you know that you breathe approximately 20,000 times each day? – it's part of a wonderfully complex system in our bodies called the respiratory system.

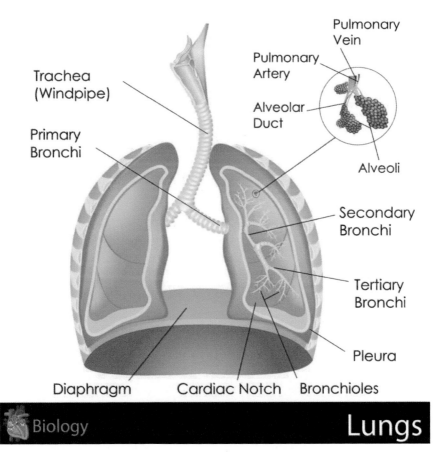

Pulmonary Vein

Pulmonary Artery

Trachea (Windpipe)

Alveolar Duct

Primary Bronchi

Alveoli

Secondary Bronchi

Tertiary Bronchi

Pleura

Diaphragm          Cardiac Notch          Bronchioles

Biology                                                   Lungs

Every system in your body has a main task. The job of the respiratory system is to help your cells breathe. Cells need oxygen to do their many jobs. Cells need energy, and in order to produce that energy, they need oxygen. The respiratory system's function is to bring in the oxygen your cells need to do all their jobs and then remove the carbon dioxide the cells burn off. That's important, because too much carbon dioxide in your body can be harmful.

You may not realize it, but your nose is a very important part of the respiratory system. You breathe in oxygen through it, and it's also the first part of your body's air filtering system. Tiny hairs and mucus inside your nose trap germs and dust when you breathe in.

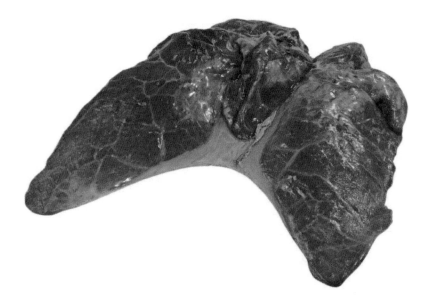

The nose connects to the **pharynx**, part of your throat. In fact, your nose and mouth, through which you also breathe in, come together at the pharynx. Your pharynx leads to your esophagus as well as to a passage for air. That makes it a very interesting body part because it's included in the digestive system as well as the respiratory system. The reason you don't get food stuck in your airways is because you have a sort of flap, called the **epiglottis**, that acts a little like a door over the air passage. The epiglottis also covers your **larynx**, sometimes called your voice box. Air vibrating on your larynx's vocal cords help you make sounds.

Your larynx leads to your trachea which connects your throat to the upper part of your chest. The

**trachea** branches out like a tree into what we call **bronchi**, and then the bronchi branch out into even smaller **bronchioles**. Right at the end of the bronchioles, you'll find **alveoli**, which are millions of tiny air sacs that make up your lungs.

Your two lungs are spongy and act as your body's air filtering system. Essentially anything that gets through your air passages that shouldn't will be filtered out by healthy lungs. When you breathe in oxygen, it goes through those millions of alveoli – there are between three and four million alveoli in each lung – and then goes into your bloodstream via your capillaries, which are very small blood vessels. The capillaries then pass back to the alveoli any carbon dioxide. The carbon dioxide leaves your body when you breathe out. It's like an exchange system.

Your lungs have five lobes, three on the right and two on the left. Can you guess why your left lung only has two lobes? Hint: think of the placement of another important organ in your body. That's right, the left lung has to leave room for your heart.

The **diaphragm** is another important part of how your body breathes. Your lungs are stretchy so they can inflate and deflate as you breathe in and out. However, they don't have a lot of muscle, and they need help to move air in and out of your body. Your diaphragm is between your chest and your abdomen, and it moves down when you breathe in, making your chest cavity bigger. Try taking a deep breath and holding it. You can note how your chest cavity rises. Then when you breathe out, your chest cavity gets smaller and the air is forced out through the lungs. Your rib muscles are part of this process too. When you exhale, both your diaphragm and rib muscles relax, changing the air pressure in your lungs. When the air pressure inside is more than the pressure outside, air gets forced out.

There are plenty of illustrations and videos online which can help you get a better visual understanding of the respiratory system. A brief animated video showing how the respiratory system works can be found here.

Doctors sometimes use something called an **ABG** test to see how healthy someone's lungs are. ABG stands for "arterial blood gases." The test measures the acidity (called the pH) of blood that is taken from an artery. It also measures how effectively the body's respiratory exchange system is working. The test measures the content and saturation of oxygen in the blood as well as the pressure of the oxygen and carbon dioxide in the blood. The pH level tells whether the blood is **acidic or basic**. The pH number can let a doctor know how effectively the lungs are working. Generally this test is done when a doctor wants to see if someone might have a serious breathing problem, or if someone is already being treated for a lung disease and the doctor wants to measure how effective a prescribed treatment already is.

## Asthma

Asthma is a long term disease that attacks the airways in a person's lungs. The airways (tubes) become inflamed and swollen, causing the circulation of air to be interrupted and difficult. Due to the inflammation, mucus (a thick bodily secretion) is often trapped in the respiratory system, creating a majority of the conflict. Though Asthma can be deadly, today's advanced medicine and technology enable those who are diagnosed with it to live fairly normal lives.

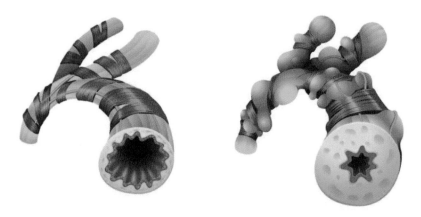

Asthma is not a constant problem for most patients. Most who suffer from it experience Asthma attacks periodically, usually in the early morning or late at night, according to most specialists. Asthma attacks usually consist of chest pains, gripping or constricting sensations in the chest area, shortness of breath and severe coughing spells. These attacks are usually triggered by environmental factors or the individual circumstances of the person experiencing them. Apart from attacks, people who have Asthma tend to experience wheezing and shortness of breath on a more regular basis.

Though Asthma can be treated, it cannot be cured completely. It is a chronic condition, which means that it affects the patient from the time of diagnosis till death. The treatment of Asthma depends on the individual patient's circumstances. Doctors have to factor in the patients' ages and what triggers the symptoms of this disease to determine which medication would best suit their needs. Some patients use inhalers with medication which opens up the airways and reduces inflammation on an as-needed basis. Others ingest pills on a daily basis to prevent attacks from occurring. Combinations of the two are often prescribed.

Asthma affects the elderly and children the most. Those who belong to different age groups can certainly be diagnosed with it, but the risk is higher for children and senior citizens. In the United States alone, close to seven million children live with this disease.

To learn more about Asthma, its symptoms and how to treat them watch this video of a panel discussion☐☐☐ on You tube:
https://www.youtube.com/watch?v=spmoKM-Q0qY

*End of Chapter Quiz*
1. Why are there only 2 lobes on the left lung?

2. Why are ABGs taken?

Answers: to make room for the heart, to determine how effective the lungs are exchanging air

**The Integumentary System**

The Integumentary system is a collection of organs that includes skin, hair and nails. This system provides a protective outer layer on the body, excretes waste through sweat, regulates temperature, and aids in the synthesis of sunlight into vitamin D. Skin is the largest body organ in mammals. If you were to stretch it flat, the skin of an average adult male would cover approximately 2 square yards and weigh close to 9 pounds.

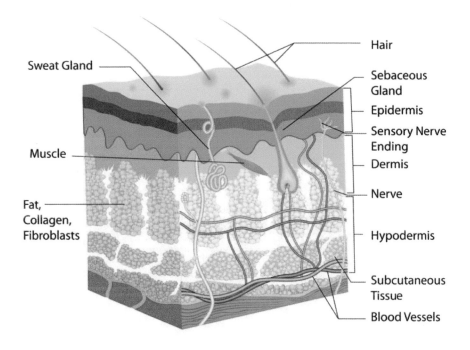

Sweat Gland

Hair

Sebaceous Gland

Epidermis

Muscle

Sensory Nerve Ending

Dermis

Nerve

Fat, Collagen, Fibroblasts

Hypodermis

Subcutaneous Tissue

Blood Vessels

Biology

# Skin Anatomy

Skin protects inner organs, muscles, bones, and tissues by acting as a waterproof suit that holds everything together. It is comprised of microscopic cells that form two distinct layers. The outer most layer is called the epidermis, the inner layer is the dermis.

The dermis contains a combination of cell types, including fibroblasts, macrophages, fat and blast cells covered by collagen filled fibers. This is also where nerve endings, blood vessels, hair roots, glands and muscle tissue are connected.

The **epidermis** grows in layers. Cells are primarily made of keratin, a protein secreted by glands called **keratinocytes**. The outer layers are collectively called the horny zone. The epidermis is thinnest on the eyelids and thickest on the soles of the feet. Growth is stimulated by shedding the horny layers.

The cells of the epidermis die and fall off, making room for new cells. A human sheds an astonishing 30,000 to 40,000 skin cells every hour, totaling more than one million over the course of a day. The skin has the ability to heal its own superficial wounds. New cells are deposited around the outside edges and gradually fill the center until healing is complete.

The skin operates with the assistance of specialized appendages. Sweat glands regulate the expulsion of wastes and temperature regulation through perspiration. The are two main types of sweat glands. Eccrine glands are found everywhere on the body. Apocrine glands are located in the armpit and pubic region. Becoming active at puberty, the perspiration is odorless until it mixes with bacteria on the surface of the skin.

One square inch of skin has more than 600 sweat glands, 1000 nerve endings, 20 blood vessels, and 60,000 pigment producing cells called melanocytes. Hair and nails are a modified type of skin, containing a similar form of keratin. While neither are necessary to sustain life, they add extra insulation and protection.

The Integumentary system has many other specialized appendages that help detect environmental temperatures, regulate other systems and allow the body to feel sensation by touch. A learning song about the anatomy and physiology of the Integumentary system can be found at

http://www.youtube.com/watch?v=MeTaBniB0ok
http://health.howstuffworks.com/skin-care/information/anatomy/shed-skin-cells.htm
http://en.wikipedia.org/wiki/Human_skin

*End of Chapter Activity*
1. Describe the structure of function of the skin.

**Eyes and Ears**

**Anatomy and Physiology**

Seeing and hearing are two senses that most of us use every day during our waking hours. It is also fascinating to learn more about how they work!

The ear is made up of three parts: the outer ear, the middle ear, and the inner ear. The main job of the outer and middle ears is to gather the sound and transmit it to the inner ear. Then the inner ear translates the sound waves into electronic impulses that can be interpreted by the brain. There is also a part of the inner ear that has the function of maintaining the body's balance.

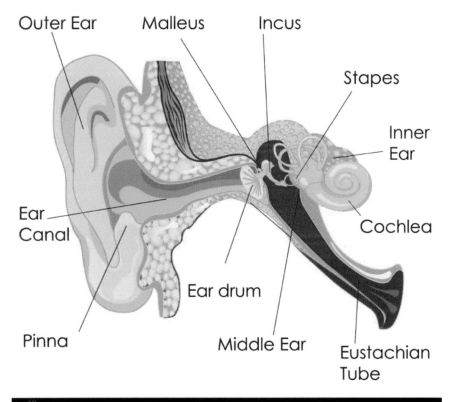

Outer Ear    Malleus    Incus

Stapes

Inner Ear

Ear Canal

Cochlea

Pinna

Ear drum

Middle Ear

Eustachian Tube

 Biology      Ear Anatomy

The outer ear is the part of the ear that we can see. The opening that is visible in the outer ear leads into the ear canal. The ear canal is about one inch long in adults and smaller in children. It separates the outer ear from the middle ear. The middle ear conducts sound to the inner ear by three very small bones called ossicles. Ossicles are the smallest bones in the human body! These bones work together to amplify sound waves. Next comes the inner ear which lies deep within the skull. It has a maze of winding passages that is referred to as the labyrinth. The front part of the inner ear is a tube that looks like a snail's shell called the cochlea and is concerned with hearing. The rear part of the inner ear is made up of semicircular canals that are responsible for the body's balance system. So hearing works by the sound waves being captured by the outer and middle ear and then translated in a way that the brain can interpret by the inner ear. Here is a good video with even more information on how the human ear works: http://www.youtube.com/watch?v=dCyz8-eAs1l.

Now onto how the eyes work. The eyes, of course, are the organs of sight. Eyes, that are located on the front, upper part of the skull, take in light and then similarly to what the ears do with sound, translate the light into electrical impulses that the brain can understand.

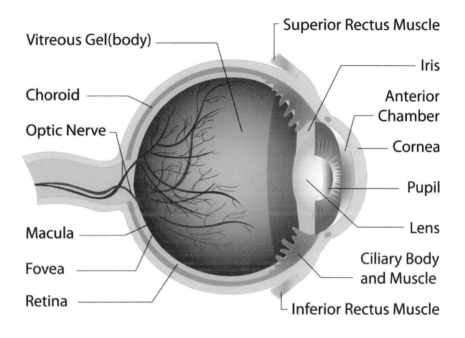

Vitreous Gel(body)

Choroid

Optic Nerve

Macula

Fovea

Retina

Superior Rectus Muscle

Iris

Anterior Chamber

Cornea

Pupil

Lens

Ciliary Body and Muscle

Inferior Rectus Muscle

Biology      Eye Anatomy

The eyes consist of eyeballs that are each set in an orbit, which is a bony socket that protects the eyeball. The eyeball also has an outer protective coat called the sclera, which is the white part of the eye. The cornea is the circular part in the front of the eye and is the main lens that performs most of the focusing. Behind the cornea is a chamber of watery fluid, and in the back of this chamber are the iris and pupil. The iris is the colored part of the eye and the pupil is the small, round, black part in the center. The pupil's diameter changes by the how much light it wants to let into the eye; it gets smaller to let in less light and bigger to let in more light. Behind the iris is the crystalline lens, which contracts to focus the light. Behind this lens is the main cavity of the eye that is filled with a clear gel. In the back of the eye is a thin layer of tissue called the retina.

The retina is made up of nerve cells called rods and cones that convert light into electrical impulses that are sent to the brain by the optic nerve. The brain then produces the final image of what we see. To watch a great video on how vision works go to: http://www.youtube.com/watch?v=gBdyU1b0ADQ.

# Human Cells

Anatomy and Physiology

Cells are the basic building blocks of life. Your body has an amazing number of cells – about 100 trillion of them! All human cells have 46 chromosomes, but different kinds of cells are responsible for different tasks.

The most common cells in your body are red blood cells. Your red blood cells are shaped like flat disks. They carry hemoglobin, a protein very rich in iron. When hemoglobin travels to the lungs, it gets oxygen. Then as your blood moves all around your body, that oxygen gets released into your tissues, essentially groups of cells that join together to accomplish a certain job.

Epithelial cells are in the business of helping to protect your body. They're found on your skin and they also make up the lining of some of your internal organs like your stomach and lungs. They help protect you from germs and they also secrete digestive juices or hormones. Hormones are what your body releases to help regulate all sorts of things from growth to moods to metabolism. Hormones make up part of what's known as the endocrine system.

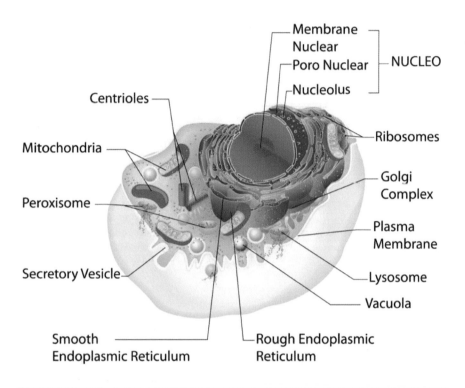

Membrane
Nuclear
Poro Nuclear     NUCLEO
Nucleolus

Centrioles

Mitochondria

Peroxisome

Secretory Vesicle

Ribosomes

Golgi
Complex

Plasma
Membrane

Lysosome

Vacuola

Smooth
Endoplasmic Reticulum

Rough Endoplasmic
Reticulum

 Biology                    Human Cell

Ovum cells are part of the female reproductive system. Females who have reached puberty produce ova, or egg cells, in their ovaries. Once a month, an egg is released from one of the ovaries, goes through the fallopian tube, and gets released into the uterus. If the egg does not get fertilized, the egg and a lining of blood that protects it will flow out of the body, in what is known as menstruation. If the egg unites with a sperm in the fallopian tube, then it becomes fertilized and will become embedded in the uterus and grow into a baby. Sperm cells, then, are part of the male reproductive system. They are the reproductive cells in males. Adult males make millions of these tiny cells per day. It takes both the sperm cells in males and the ovum cells in females to make a baby.

Bone cells help your bones grow and also repair when they're broken. Since your body needs bones for support and movement, bone cells are vital. There are three main kinds: osteoblasts, osteocytes and osteoclasts. That last kind of cell is especially crucial in younger people, because osteoclasts help to shape bones as they grow.

# ANATOMY OF HUMAN CELLS

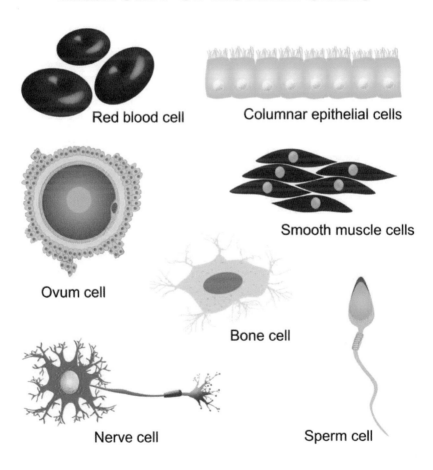

Red blood cell

Columnar epithelial cells

Ovum cell

Smooth muscle cells

Bone cell

Nerve cell

Sperm cell

Nerve cells are not only important but unique in that you had all the nerve cells you'd ever have when you were born. Other cells, like your blood cells, replenish themselves often, but nerve cells (or neurons) don't reproduce. Nerve cells help our bodies receive and pass messages so that our bodies can function properly.

The nervous system helps your body control its smooth muscles. Our skeletal muscles can contract and we can control their movement. But our smooth muscles, like our stomach and intestine walls, move without us needing to tell them to. Smooth muscle cells work together to help those involuntary actions, like digesting food, occur when and how they should.

*End of Chapter Quiz*
1. Where are osteoclasts and osteoblasts located?

2. What is the function of epithelial cells?


Answers: bones, healing located in skin and lining of organs


**Thank you so much for reading!  We wish you success in your studies of the human body!**


**We have worked very hard to publish this book.  Please leave a kind review in Amazon if you enjoy this ebook.  If you have suggestions for us to improve please let us know in kind words so that we can improve our teaching resources.**

Printed in Great Britain
by Amazon.co.uk, Ltd.,
Marston Gate.